IN-LINE SKATING

Jed Morgan

FRANKLIN WATTS
LONDON • SYDNEY

First published in 2005 by
Franklin Watts
96 Leonard Street
London
EC2A 4XD

Franklin Watts Australia
45–51 Huntley Street
Alexandria, NSW 2015

© Franklin Watts 2005

Series editor: Adrian Cole
Series design: Pewter Design Associates
Art director: Jonathan Hair
Picture researcher: Sophie Hartley

A CIP catalogue record for this book is available from the British Library.

ISBN: 0 7496 5821 5

Printed in Malaysia

The author and publisher would like to thank the following people for their contribution to the production of this book: Steve and Jill Behr at Stockfile (www.stockfile.co.uk), June Anderson at K2 (UK) Ltd (www.k2skates.com), Harry Scott Rollerblade (UK) Ltd (www.rollerblade.com), Kris Thomas (www.zephyradventures.com), Deborah L. Wallis, Director and Curator of the National Museum of Roller Skating, USA (www.rollerskatingmuseum.com), Peter Krüger, Chairman of the Inline-Basketball in DRIV (German Inline and Skate Association), Berlin (www.tsc-berlin.de/inline-basketball.htm), Andrew Padden (www.womens-ih.co), Stephen Olner at Digital Chilli (www.digitalchilli.net.uk), Tanao Terra (www.pari-roller.com), Andreas Kolattek (www.citiskate.co.uk) and the staff at www.berlin-marathon.com.

Acknowledgements:
The Publisher acknowledges all © products shown within this title as the property of their respective owners. Steve Bardens/Action Plus: 5t, 8b. DPPI/Action Plus: 27b. Courtesy www.citiskate.co.uk: 19t. Courtesy K2 (UK) Limited: 4bl, 7t & b, 9l, tr & br, 10t, 11tl, 12t, 16t, 26. Photo by Frank Manischewski: 19b. National Museum of Roller Skating, Lincoln, Nebraska: 4t. © Stephen Olner: 18. © Andrew Padden: 29 (inset). © Pari-Roller: 11tr, 16b. AGF/Rex Features: 27t. Alisdair Macdonald/ Rex Features: 15b. Courtesy Rollerblade International:4br, 5b, 6-7, 8t, 9cr, 10b, 20r, 21b, 22b, 23t, 25b. © SCC-Running: 17b. © Stockfile/Steven Behr: 11b, 12b, 13t & b, 14t, 15t, 20l, 21tl, tc & tr, 22t, 23bl & br, 24t, 25tl, tc & tr. © Stockfile/Jess Dyrenforth: 24b, 28, 29 (main). © Superstock: Cover, 14b. Courtesy Zephyr Adventures www.zephyradventures.com: 17t.

Contents

World of in-line skating

In-line skates allow you to reach mind-boggling speeds, perform amazing tricks or just cruise around the park. They give you incredible freedom to explore the world around you.

To the limit

In 1760 Joseph Merlin wore in-line skates in public for the first time at a party in London. Unfortunately, he had forgotten to do two things: to practise skating and to invent a brake for his new skates! He went flying across the ballroom and slammed into a mirror.

Early in-line skating

A Belgian, Joseph Merlin, developed the earliest-known in-line skates in 1760 to practise ice-skating on dry land. By 1819 M. Petitbled from France patented a three-wheeled version (right), and an English skate called the 'Rolito' followed in 1823. Forty years later, a new roller skate with two parallel sets of wheels changed everything. They were easier to use and in-line skating went out of fashion.

The 'Petitbled' had three rubber wheels mounted in a line on a wooden frame.

(Left) Aggressive skating (page 9) is a fast growing form of in-line skating.
(Right) The logo of the Rollerblade Corporation.

In-line reborn

Modern in-line skates can be traced back to 1979. Two ice-hockey players, Scott and Brennan Olson from Minneapolis, USA, experimented with an old in-line skate. In 1980 they started a company to produce an in-line skate they called a 'Rollerblade'. By 1984 they had sold their company. An improved version of their Rollerblade called 'Lightning TRS' became the first truly popular in-line skate.

> *In-line street hockey is a great way to combine sport with in-line skating skills.*

Around the world

In-line skating spread rapidly across the USA. By the end of the 1990s there were over 32 million in-line skaters in the USA alone — more than the entire population of Scandinavia! As the design improved further, in-line skates were marketed for exercise or racing, and for the fast-growing sport of in-line hockey. By 1997 in-line skating had become a billion pound worldwide sport and it's still growing today.

FROM THE EDGE

'...all in-line skaters are united by a common experience: the thrill and easy feeling of having seemingly frictionless wheels on their feet, and the freedom of movement, expression and speed in-line skating lets them achieve.' Michael Zaidman, Director and Curator of the National Museum of Roller Skating (1996–99), Lincoln, USA. The museum collects, preserves and researches everything to do with in-line and roller skating history.

Know your skates

In-line skates look similar, but there are many different types. This Rollerblade Lightning 05 is a high-performance skate, but has many features shared with other skates.

Liner — PFS PROfessional LITE with Coolmax© technology

SHELL (outer boot that gives the skate its shape)
* Design — most shells are made with types of plastic, including ballistic nylon. These are combined with other materials, such as carbon fibre, to provide more flexibility. These are called composite shells.
* Air vents — increase airflow in the boot.
* Cuff — helps transfer power from your leg to the skate.

BRAKE
Recreational in-line skates are fitted with a brake. This is normally on the heel of the right-hand skate. It consists of a brake support and replaceable rubber pad.

Shell — Fibreglass-charged plastic with Soft Touch© finish

WHEEL FRAME
This holds the wheels in place, gives the skate stiffness and control and is normally made from aluminium or synthetic materials, such as polycarbonate. Aggressive frames are fitted with additional grind plates.

Wheel frame — Litespeed (285mm)

LINER *(inner boot that fits around your foot)*
✱ Design — liners are made from synthetic materials. They must fit well, and some even shape themselves to your feet! Look for ones with thick padding on the toes to help absorb hits.
✱ Hygiene — liners can be removed from the shell. Aggressive skates usually have an anti-bacterial liner to reduce odours.

CLOSURE
In-line skates have different closure systems, including laces, zips, Velcro straps and buckles — sometimes all of the above!

Cool science

Durometer is a manufacturing industry hardness test for plastics. Different ratings are used on in-line skate wheels to indicate the hardness of the plastic (usually polyurethane) used to make them. The highest (hardest) rating is 100A and the lowest (softest) 74A, although most skaters use wheels with a rating of between 78A and 82A (left).

Closure — Quick slide eyelets, lacelock, powerstrap, zip lace cover and locking buckle

HOT HINT

Don't forget your bearings! These steel micro-balls fit between the wheel and the axle. They keep your wheels moving smoothly.

Micro-bearings

Wheels — 82mm / 82A Rollerblade LITE HP

WHEELS
Wheels come in different sizes and degrees of hardness. Standard wheels are 76–80mm in diameter.
✱ Soft wheels give more grip and a softer, slower ride, but also wear down quickly.
✱ Hard wheels last longer, but give a more bumpy ride with less grip.

In-line for all

Whatever your style, there is an in-line skate for you. Not all skates are suitable for all uses though, so choosing the right one is important. In general you will get what you pay for.

Recreational skates

Standard recreational skates are the most common in-line skates with lots of entry-level designs. They normally have all the standard features shown on pages 6–7. They are good general-purpose skates for beginners to start off with. Most can be upgraded with different wheels and bearings.

Toe heel glide on recreational skates.

HOT HINT

'Try hiring a few pairs before you buy. Some skate shops will even take the hire cost off the price of a new pair of skates. The main thing to remember is don't let yourself be pressurised into buying skates that aren't right for you.'
Jean Couderc, in-line skater from France

Hockey skates

These have smaller, harder wheels to allow greater agility. Many of them are made with soft leather or synthetic shells. Better skates will have no liner and will use laces rather than straps as fastenings. Although hockey skates are great on purpose-made rinks they give a bumpy ride on general outdoor surfaces.

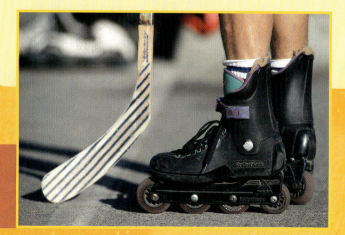
Hockey skates can be expensive. Many amateur in-line hockey players wear hard-wearing recreational skates like these, instead.

Speed skates

Speed skates look very different to other in-line skates. They have a low-cut boot, which doesn't have a liner, and a longer wheel frame with five instead of four wheels. They are very light and use materials, such as aluminium or carbon fibre (lightweight but strong), for the wheel frame.

Speed skates are designed to be as lightweight as possible.

Aggressive skates

These skates are the in-line heavyweights — tough and virtually indestructible. They are specifically designed to take the serious hits and falls that are part of street skating. All aggressive skates have additional armour on the toe caps and around the ankles, and an extra thick liner. They have four small wheels, usually about 55mm, that are protected by hardwearing grind plates for serious rail slides (left). Most aggressive skaters customise their skates to fit their style.

Get geared up

In-line skating can be a dangerous sport — especially for beginners. It is important that you have the right gear to protect yourself against injuries while looking cool, too.

Helmet

Your head is the most important part of your body. Even at slow speeds a fall can cause serious damage, so get a helmet! You will find a variety to choose from depending on your skate style, but the most important thing is to make sure you get one that fits. Most helmets come with adjustable pads and straps.

Skating with friends. Learn from your experiences — especially when it comes to sharing safety tips.

HOT HINT

'Get a helmet! I mean it! You can break your arms or legs and still live. You don't want to break your head'.
Tony Chen, skatefaq website

Body gear

Wearing body gear is a decision you have to make. You should wear wrist guards (above), elbow pads and knee pads (and a helmet). However, as you become more experienced, you may decide to wear only some of these. Buy the best quality gear you can afford — and make sure it fits. Badly fitting gear offers you little protection and can be uncomfortable.

Be seen

If you are going to skate at night then make sure you can be seen by drivers, pedestrians or cyclists. To help you really stand out wear bright-coloured clothing, a reflective band around your arm or body and skate lights.

Reflective bands are a simple way to stand out from the crowd.

Hanging out at the skatepark. Some skaters say they don't wear a helmet because of the heat. Buy one that is a light colour (to reflect the heat) or with extra air vents.

Clothing

You can wear almost anything to in-line skate; it depends on your style. When starting out, long-sleeved tops and long trousers are best as they offer extra protection when you fall — but may not stop you getting road rash completely! Most aggressive skaters wear loose-fitting clothing. Many recreational skaters wear clothing made of Lycra. In cold weather, fleece clothing and a hoodie can help to keep you warm. A lightweight waterproof jacket can protect you against the wind and rain.

HOT HINT

'Some people don't like wearing [body] gear... It's down to you to stay safe. Whether you skate in a park or on the street, you should always wear wrist guards and a helmet.'
Fernandez H. Sergio, UK

11

Get ready to go

In-line skates are an extension of your body. They help you to glide along, but it's still your muscles that get you moving. Because of this it is important that you warm up first.

A good stretch

Stretching prepares your muscles for the activity you want them to do. A stretch should be a slow, gradual movement and not sudden. When you feel your muscles go tense, stop stretching and hold that position for about 15 seconds. Repeat each stretch several times and make sure you do the same stretches on both sides of your body.

Stretching will help to improve your striding and jumps.

Hamstring stretch (left leg).

Hamstring muscle

Sit on the floor with both legs straight out in front of you. Bring one foot up towards your groin, but keep the other straight. Now slowly reach with both hands towards your furthest foot until you feel the tension in your hamstring.

Stomach muscles

The best way to exercise your stomach muscles (there are many) is to do rotations. Stand with your feet apart and keep your body upright. Gently rotate your upper body at the waist (keeping your pelvis facing forwards) until you feel tension in your stomach muscles. Remember not to overstretch.

Skate maintenance

A good skater should make sure their skates are in good working order before they head out. Replace worn wheels or brakes and lubricate any noisy bearings. Remember to take a repair kit and spares with you. And don't forget water and some snacks, too.

Rotating left and right helps to improve your flexibility and stomach strength.

HOT HINT

Do your skate maintenance at the end of a day's skating. That way your skates are always ready to go when your friends call around.

2.

3.

4.

5.

6.

1.

Repairs on the run
If you are skating away from home you should carry a few essential spares with you in a shoulder pack (1) or similar. These should include: a skate tool (2 and 3, normally supplied with your skates), some lubricant (4) and spare parts — bearings (5) and wheels (6).

Play it safe

In-line skating is exciting, but if you're not careful, a great day out can turn sour. Learning to play it safe can prevent such problems and make your experience more enjoyable.

Lessons are available for in-line skaters of any age.

HOT HINT

Some newbies have a fear of falling. Practise falling over on grass — even without skates on — to get used to the feeling. You're going to be doing a lot of it in the future!

Look after yourself

Even with safety gear you will fall over. That's why it is a good idea to try out your first moves on a soft surface, such as short grass. Take advice and lessons from more-experienced skaters or instructors. This will help reduce the chances of you causing serious injuries when you first start out (see pages 20–21).

You won't be performing like this on the halfpipe in your first session. Get to grips with the basics first.

When you are ready

Don't be pressurised into doing in-line moves that you are not comfortable with. Remember, even the most experienced skaters were once newbies themselves! To be a really good in-line skater takes time, practice, confidence and patience. You should only tackle new moves once you feel ready.

Watch the sun

Nothing beats cruising or tricking outside on a hot summer's day. The sun has hidden dangers though, and can burn uncovered skin and dehydrate you very quickly. Wear sun block or cover bare skin, and make sure you stop for regular water breaks. Sunglasses don't just make you look cool either; they will protect your eyes from glare.

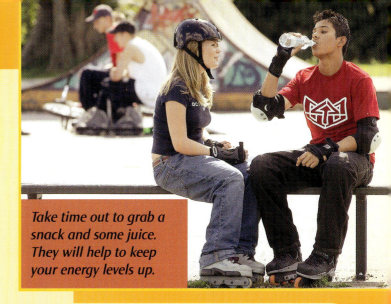

Take time out to grab a snack and some juice. They will help to keep your energy levels up.

Look ahead

With your new-found freedom there is a temptation to go too fast too soon. It is really important to make sure you can stop — just remember what happened to Joseph Merlin (see page 4)! Always look and think ahead, and slow down before you actually need to stop. This will prevent injuries caused by coming to an abrupt stop, and also make your brakes last longer.

Think of others

You must be responsible and think of those around you when you are skating — a rude and dangerous skater gives all skaters a bad name. A skater travelling at speed in a busy place can be a scary sight. You should always give way to pedestrians and let them know you are coming — if they can't see you, simply say 'pass please'. If there are young children or animals where you are skating then you must take extra special care — they are sure to run out in front of you!

HOT HINT

'Watch out for sudden changes in the pavement surface. One minute you can be striding along flat concrete, and the next picking yourself up out of a hole!' Sunny Tobias, California, USA

Always obey traffic signals, and never skate in the road.

FROM THE EDGE

Safety tips for in-line street skaters:

* Always wear protective gear: a helmet, wrist guards, knee and elbow pads
* Learn in-line skating basics such as stopping and turning before going out
* Stay away from water, oil, debris or sand on the ground and uneven or broken pavements
* Observe all traffic regulations
* Move to the right of pedestrians, cyclists and other skaters to pass them

Just For Fun

In-line skating is a competitive worldwide sport, but for the majority of skaters it's simply a way to hang out and have fun.

Free Fun

Once you have your basic gear you can skate for free if you choose. Cycle routes and local parks are particularly good places to go, but some may not allow skating so check first. Many towns are even building their own public skateparks to encourage skaters off the streets.

Private session

Private skateparks have larger layouts than public ones, with ramps, bowls and rails for you to practise on. They are a great place to meet and learn from more-experienced skaters. You may have to pay a session fee, but as many skateparks have areas set aside for beginners, it's worth spending the money.

Grinding at the skatepark. Paying out for a session at a park is well worth the money.

FROM THE EDGE

Many cities now have weekly meets where in-line skaters gather to socialise and skate. The 'Pari-Roller' is the most famous of these skate meetings and takes place in Paris, France, where thousands of skaters meet for a late night skate through the city. 'France is the perfect destination for a skating holiday. It is the home of the world famous Paris Friday Night Skate, which every skater should experience at least once in their life.' Kathie Fry, editor of www.skatelog.com

FROM THE EDGE

In 1997, Zephyr Adventures (www.zephyradventures.com) was the first company in the world to organise holidays for in-line skaters. People aged 11–72 take part in tours held in many places including Florida, Germany and Switzerland (right). 'This skating trip rates as one of the best vacations I have ever had.' Skater from the USA

In-line experiences

In-line holidays and tours are a great way to get more out of skating and explore new places all over the world. You could explore Korea's volcanic Jeju island, skate through the heart of New York or tour through the rolling landscapes of Switzerland.

The Berlin skate marathon is the biggest in the world. In 2004 it was won by Roland Ehmann (men) and Stephanie Schubert (women).

In-line events

In-line events provide the perfect opportunity to meet other skaters, check out the latest fashions and gear, and take part in competitions. There are also skate marathons or half marathons, which take place around the world from Germany to Tahiti. Skate magazines, shops and websites normally advertise events and there is almost certainly something happening near you.

In-line sports

Modern in-line skates were developed as a way to practise ice hockey. By 1995 in-line hockey had its own World Championship. Other sports, including football and basketball, soon followed.

In-line hockey

In-line hockey is one of the world's fastest-growing sports, with competitions at local, national and international level. However, most in-line hockey is played locally in parks, sports halls or ice centres. Each team has five players and must try to hit the puck into the other team's goal. The first FIRS (International Roller Sports Federation) World In-line Hockey Championship was held in Chicago in 1995. It takes place in a different country every year. In 2002, the women's FIRS World Championship was held for the first time.

To the limit

FIRS (International Roller Sports Federation) was set up in 1925. It is the international governing body that incorporates both roller and in-line sports. FIRS works closely with the International Olympic Committee. Many people believe it will help to establish in-line hockey as an Olympic sport.

In-line hockey games are held on 'plastic' and on the 'street'. All of them are fast and furious.

RollerSoccer (In-line Football)

Back in 1995 Zack Phillips, a keen in-line skater from San Francisco, was skating when he kicked a football that crossed his path. He came up with a new idea and within weeks Zack was organising the first in-line football matches with his friends. Each team had five players and they created rules similar to football, but with some borrowed from in-line hockey, too.

Today RollerSoccer is spreading rapidly, with leagues in the UK, Pakistan, Brazil and Australia, as well as across the USA. In 2004, the RollerSoccer World Cup was held in London, UK. The tournament was won by Germany (South).

FROM THE EDGE

'Players from a variety of sports backgrounds have been able to excel at RollerSoccer. Some of the best players could hardly skate when they started.' RollerSoccer International Federation website (www.rollersoccer.com)

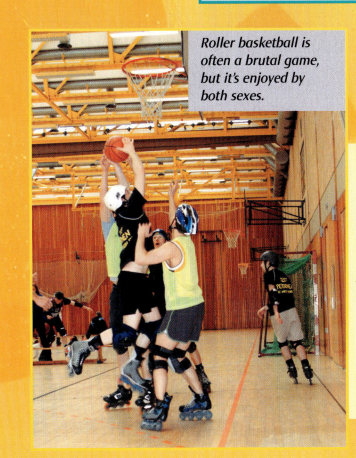

Roller basketball is often a brutal game, but it's enjoyed by both sexes.

Roller basketball (In-line basketball)

Basketball is already a fast and exciting sport, but add in-line skates and the speed and thrills are doubled! An American basketball player called Tom LaGarde founded in-line basketball in 1992. It is centred around New York where there are regular weekly games, but the sport has also spread to other American cities. Germany, the Netherlands, Pakistan, Brazil and Portugal also have a growing number of players.

Basic skills

Most beginners are itching to get going, but it is well worth spending some time learning the basic skills. The best way to learn is to take lessons, but some basic starter skills will help you on your way.

Stay relaxed

Get used to standing on your skates before you try any moves — and stay relaxed! Stand upright with your feet shoulder-width apart and your knees slightly bent. Lean gently forwards from your ankles onto the balls of your feet. Keep your shoulders relaxed, your head up, and stretch your arms out in front of you to help balance. This is the ready position. Practise this starting position until you feel comfortable.

HOT HINT

Don't forget to take a break. Just sit out of the action for 5 or 10 minutes every 30 minutes of skating — you'll find it easier to keep your energy levels up.

First strides

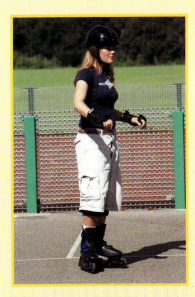

1. From the ready position bring your heels together and point your toes outwards. You should now be on the inside edges of your skates in the V position.

2. Slowly roll one skate forwards and gently push off with the other. This pushing movement is called a stroke. As you make a stroke, move your weight forwards onto the front skate.

3. As you move, lift the stroke skate (the back one) off the ground and glide forwards. A stroke and glide together is a stride — the basic in-line move. As your stroke skate comes back to the ground bring it parallel with your front skate and glide forwards in the ready position.

Stopping

Learning to stop is the most important skill you need. When gliding forward in the ready position move your braking skate forwards until its back wheel is level with the front wheel of the other skate. This is the scissor position. Lift the toe of your braking skate so the brake drags. Lean forward slightly at the waist and straighten your braking leg to increase the pressure on the braking skate. Keep your other leg bent at the knee until you come to a stop.

Moving on

Once you have mastered the basic skills it is time to move on to some more advanced skills. These will allow you to begin serious in-line skating and are the starting point for learning in-line tricks.

Make that first turn

The first turn to learn is the 'A-frame turn'.

✴ Glide forward in the ready position and allow your skates to move apart into an 'A-frame'.

✴ To turn, increase the pressure on one skate by pressing down with your toes and pointing the skate in the direction you wish to turn. If you put pressure on the left skate you will turn right. Keep your body relaxed and remember to look ahead. Complete the turn by bringing your feet back into the ready position.

'Slaloming' around bollards is a great way to practise turning.

Parallel turns are a more advanced way of turning. They help you to avoid trouble by turning quickly.

Parallel turns

To parallel turn you need to glide with your skates in a narrow scissor position.

✴ Your lead (steering skate) will decide your turning direction. To turn left your left skate should lead.

✴ Gently point your toes in the direction you wish to turn. This will put your skates onto their edges, ready to make the turn.

✴ Now, twist your body from the waist in the direction of the turn and look where you are turning.

✴ Complete the turn by returning your body and knees back to the centre.

If you can't get a move right, try it with some friends. They can often spot where you're going wrong.

Stepping down

1. To go down large steps it is best to stop and step down. For smaller kerb-height steps you can slowly skate off them. To do this, approach the step in a narrow scissors position and at a slight angle.

2. Keep your weight in the centre of your skates and just glide off. Your knees and ankles will cushion your landing so keep them bent forwards and relaxed.

Advanced tricks

Most tricks take a long time to master. It is a good idea to take lessons in how to do them. This page shows three of the most popular tricks.

Toe heel glide

This is a fun trick that looks cool and can really improve your balance.

✱ Skate in a wide scissor position along a smooth surface. Tip your non-braking skate up so that you are gliding on its rear wheel.

✱ Point your braking skate so that you stand on the front wheel or toe.

✱ Keep looking ahead, use your arms to balance and keep your knees bent. This is a toe heel glide. Start off slowly until you become confident.

Fabiola da Silva moving to soul X grind a halfpipe rail.

Grinding

Grinds are a big part of aggressive skating. The soul grind is considered to be one of the easier grinds — but there are lots of others to learn. To soul grind a rail:

✱ Get up some speed and jump up high enough to fix a position on the rail.

✱ Land both feet at the same time, with the outside of your back foot parallel with the rail (the soul position) and your front foot facing forward (frontside).

✱ Bend your back foot (or 'soul' foot) to maintain your balance as you grind along the rail.

The jump

1. As you approach the ramp you should be in the ready position with your knees well bent and your body leaning forward from the waist. You can push off the lip of the ramp to give you extra height (air).

2. When you take off, pull your knees into your chest and swing your arms upwards. This will help you get more air. To stay in control mid-jump, hold your knees up against your chest in a tuck position. As you exit the jump, lower your legs, keep your knees bent and put your arms out in front of you.

3. Look ahead to where you are going to land and start moving your feet into a scissor position ready for landing. Your strongest leg should be at the rear. As your skates touch down, allow your legs to bend. They will help to absorb the impact. Once you have landed you can safely return to the ready position.

FROM THE EDGE

'If you're just starting out, getting a nice tuck may be difficult. Keep working at it though. It will really increase the height you achieve.' Scott Weintraub, jumping tutorial at skatefaq website

HOT HINT

'Tricks are not just to show your skills, but are a good test of balance and will help further develop your all-round skating.' Mark Heeley, author of '1st In-Line'

Get serious!

For most people, in-line skating is just a fun way to keep fit and spend time with friends. However, with ambition and a lot of determination there are no limits to how far you could go.

Begin at home

In-line skating is a tough sport and you need to be very fit and know enough tricks to really do well. Practice is the best way to make it to the top, so spend at least 30 minutes a day on your skates. Find out about clubs in your local area and join one. There you can improve your skills by watching others and sharing tips. Clubs also give you a chance to try different in-line activities so you can find out what style you enjoy the most.

Watching other more experienced in-line skaters can give you ideas to develop your own moves and style.

Speed skating in Rome, Italy. Skating in a line (drafting) improves the speed of the skaters behind the leader.

A world event

In-line skating is a world sport and it's every serious skater's dream to appear in a world event. Start by entering local club competitions. All skaters start this way and then gradually compete at regional, national and then international events. Another good way forward is to watch a major competition if it comes near to where you live. Not only is this a thrilling sight in itself, but a fantastic way to learn from the very best in the sport!

To the limit

The ultimate speed in-line skater is Theresa Cliff Ryan. She has won 48 World Championship medals including 25 golds — more than any other skater! Theresa started racing when she was just 15, winning 3 gold medals in her first year. She is one of the best in-line skaters of all time.

Go for gold!

At the moment, in-line skating is mainly limited to its own international events. In 1992 in-line hockey was a show sport at the Barcelona Olympics. It was very popular with the crowds and there is hope that it will soon become an official Olympic event. In-line events, including hockey, speed and figure skating, are already part of the Pan American Games. These are held every four years between the 42 nations of the Americas. The same in-line events will also be part of the World Games in 2005. Maybe by the time you reach your best it will be part of the Olympic Games — the world's biggest sporting event.

In-line events are held across the world and draw massive crowds.

27

Meet the pros

To become an in-line pro you will have to put in lots of practice and be very determined. It is hard work, but if you make it you will become a familiar name to thousands of fans.

Grabbing sponsorship

Sponsorship is a big deal — it helps great in-line skaters become stars by providing them with the best gear. Free goodies don't just fall from the sky, though. You have to earn them by being a great skater with a cool attitude. Once you've achieved a good position in local competitions, ask at your local skate shop. You never know, they might give you some handouts in exchange for putting their shop logo on your event jersey. Keep skating and you just never know — maybe skate fans could be putting posters of you on their wall.

To the limit
RIDER PROFILE:

Fabiola da Silva from Brazil has appeared in 9 of the 10 X-Games (XG) events and has won eight medals — seven of them gold! She is the best woman in the world at aggressive in-line and is now challenging the men, too. In the 2004 XG she came sixth in the combined men's and women's aggressive in-line vert final.

To the limit

RIDER PROFILES:

Aggressive in-line skating is currently dominated by Japanese brothers, Eito and Takeshi Yasutoko. Eito is the elder brother and the only male skater to have ever won three gold medals in the XG in 1999, 2000 and 2003. He lost out in 2004 to his younger brother Takeshi who added the gold to his five other XG medals. The Yasutoko family are all skaters and have been nicknamed the 'first skate family of Japan'. They are known for trying exciting new tricks like Eito's 1440 flat spin (four mid-air horizontal spins!) and Takeshi's double Viking flip (right).

Takeshi Yasutoko's trademark double Viking flip has helped to build his skate style. Developing trademark tricks is just one way to get yourself noticed.

The Canadian women's in-line hockey team celebrate their victory in 2004.

Hockey giants

The USA and Canada are the teams to beat in in-line hockey. In the 2004 FIRS World Championship these two teams competed for the gold medal in both the men's and women's events. The USA men successfully defended their gold medal, but in the women's final Canada beat the USA to claim the gold. The Czech Republic won the bronze for the women and Italy claimed bronze for the men.

Jargon buster

ballistic nylon — a type of very tough plastic, used to make the shell of some in-line skates.

bearings — steel micro-balls enclosed within a ring that fits between a skate wheel and the axle. Without them the wheels would grind to a halt.

carbon fibre — a material added to skate shells to improve flexibility.

cuffs — strong, plastic ankle supports that help to transfer power from your legs to your skates.

durometer — a rating scale used to describe the hardness of plastic, ranging from 74A to 100A.

gliding — moving forward without pumping your legs.

grinding — moving along coping, a rail or kerb. There are many different grinds.

grind plates — flat bars usually made of tough plastic or metal that are fitted to aggressive skates to protect the frame and wheels and help grind.

FIRS — (International Roller Sports Federation) the in-line sports governing body.

frontside — a type of grind in which you jump clockwise onto an object with both feet positioned at 90 degrees to it.

halfpipe — a 'U'-shaped ramp usually made of steel or wood.

Lycra — the tradename for an elastic fabric that is used to make sportswear.

newbie — a beginner or someone new to the in-line skate scene.

polycarbonate — a very strong plastic used to make in-line skate frames and other parts.

road rash — a graze usually sustained from scraping along the pavement after a fall.

slalom — the combination of several left and right parallel turns, one after the other.

sponsorship — when a skater is given money by a in-line team or manufacturer to race in return for promoting their products.

stroke — pushing off from one skate to the other.

stride — the combination of a stroke and glide.

X grind — a grind when both feet are 'souling' from opposite sides (so you form a X).

vert — a halfpipe that becomes vertical at the top.

Find out more

Every effort has been made by the Publishers to ensure that these websites contain no inappropriate or offensive material. However, because of the nature of the Internet, it is impossible to guarantee that the contents of these sites will not be altered. We strongly advise that Internet access is supervised by a responsible adult.

www.aggressive.com

This website is packed with product reviews, trick and skill guides, links, photos and a wealth of information to help you keep healthy and stay injury-free. It also has its own skater's log featuring music and games from the aggressive skating scene.

www.skatelog.com

Internet-dominating website edited by Kathie Fry containing almost everything you need to know about in-line skating. Check out the guides, reviews, gallery and many other topics to get you skating.

www.rollerskatingmuseum.com

Website of the National Museum of Roller Skating features on-line exhibits and history. The museum is committed to enriching the experience of all skaters.

www.k2skates.com

Up to date event reviews, in-line skating links, athlete profiles — plus the latest skates, gear and accessories from K2.

www.rollerblading.com.au

Massive Australian in-line skating website filled with the latest news, competitions, guides, reviews and tips.

www.rollerblade.com

Check out the latest skate designs, specifications and tips on the website from the Rollerblade Corporation. It also has links to the 'skate in school' programme based in the USA.

www.iisa.org

Website for the International In-line Skating Association. It includes in-line skating news, skate care tips and lots of information to help you buy the right skates and gear.

www.rollersoccer.com

Find out more about RollerSoccer on this dedicated website, featuring the history of the game and plenty of hints and tips to get you started.

Index